YAHOSHUA HA'
MASHIAKH
יהושע המשיח

TELA = LAMB

- **1st Month:** Abib
- **Symbol:** Ram
- **Mazzaroth Name:** Tela
- **Ruling Angel:** Adnar'EL

March 2023

ABIB / אביב

The Ram
The first symbol of YAHOSHUA, as the "Lamb slain from the foundation of the world." (Rev 13:8) He is the leader of the sheep, adorned with a crown (horns). This Mazzaroth represents strength, sacrifice and purity.

First Yom Reshon Sunday	Second Yom Shenee Monday	Third Yom Shelishi Tuesday	Fourth Yom Rebi'ee (Midst of Week) Wednesday	Fifth Yom Khamishee Thursday	Sixth Yom Shi'shee Friday	Sabbath Shabbath Saturday
			1 Adar 17	**2** Adar 18	**3** Adar 19	**4** Adar 20
5 Adar 21	**6** Adar 22	**7** Adar 23	**8** Adar 24	**9** Adar 25	**10** Adar 26	**11** Adar 27
12 Adar 28	**13** Adar 29	**14** Adar 30	**15** SPRING EQUINOX	**16** ABIB 1 New Years Levi's Birth	**17** Abib 2	**18** Abib 3
19 Abib 4	**20** Abib 5	**21** Abib 6	**22** Abib 7	**23** Abib 8	**24** Abib 9	**25** Abib 10
26 Abib 11	**27** Abib 12	**28** Abib 13	**29** Crucifixion Passover Eve Abib 14	**30** Passover Khag Matzah Abib 15	**31** Khag Matzah Abib 16	

ENOCH THE SCRIBE
חנוך הסופר

SHOR = BULL

- **2nd Month:** Iyar
- **Symbol:** Bull
- **Mazzaroth Name:** Shor
- **Ruling Angel:** Yeshusha'EL

April 2023

Iyar / אייר

The Bull
The Bull symbolizes the leadership and the strength of YAHOSHUA. The Hebrew letter ALEPH is the figure of the Bulls head. The Messiah is the Aleph and Taw. "I am Aleph and Taw, saith YAHOWAH." (Rev 1:8)

First Yom Reshon Sunday	Second Yom Shenee Monday	Third Yom Shelishi Tuesday	Fourth Yom Rebi'ee (Midst of Week) Wednesday	Fifth Yom Khamishee Thursday	Sixth Yom Shi'shee Friday	Sabbath Shabbath Saturday
The Firstborn Birthright and The Bull "AND LO, A BULL UPON THE EARTH, WITH TWO GREAT HORNS, AND AN EAGLE'S WINGS UPON HIS BACK; AND WE WISHED TO SEIZE HIM, BUT COULD NOT. BUT YOSEPH CAME, AND SEIZED HIM, AND ASCENDED UP WITH HIM ON HIGH." (NAPHTALI 5:6-7)						**1** YAHOSHUA'S Resurrection Abib 17
2 Omer 1 Khag Matzah Abib 18	**3** Omer 2 Khag Matzah Abib 19	**4** Omer 3 Khag Matzah Abib 20	**5** Omer 4 Passover End Abib 21	**6** Omer 5 Abib 22	**7** Martyrdom of James Zebedee Apostle of Yahoshua	**8** 1st Sabbath Abib 24
9 Omer 8 Abib 25	**10** Omer 9 Abib 26	**11** Omer 10 Abib 27	**12** Omer 11 Abib 28	**13** Omer 12 Abib 29	**14** Omer 13 Abib 30	**15** IYAR 1 2nd Sabbath
16 Omer 15 Iyar 2	**17** Omer 16 Iyar 3	**18** Omer 17 Iyar 4	**19** Martyrdom of Mark Apostle of Yahoshua	**20** Omer 19 Iyar 6	**21** Omer 20 Iyar 7	**22** 3rd Sabbath Iyar 8
23 Omer 22 Iyar 9	**24** Omer 23 Iyar 10	**25** Omer 24 Iyar 11	**26** Omer 25 Iyar 12	**27** Omer 26 Iyar 13	**28** Omer 27 Iyar 14	**29** Omer 28 Iyar 15
30 Omer 29 Iyar 16						

WHAT IS THE
MAZZAROTH?

In the northern slopes of the Gilboa mountains of Israel, there rests the remains of a sixth century synagogue called Beit Alfa (אלפא בית). This building once housed a congregation of Israelites who kept the commandments of ELOHIM and the faith of YAHOSHUA. After lying dormant for centuries and covered by the sands of time, YAHOWAH in His infinite wisdom and foresight allowed this synagogue to be rediscovered and excavated in 1928; followed by a second round of excavations in 1968. Our MASHIAKH said "There is nothing covered, that shall not be revealed; neither hid, that shall not be known." This synagogue has been brought to light in these latter days as a testament and witness to show that not only did the early assemblies of YAHOSHUA keep the law, but they also kept the Enoch Calendar.

Assorted on the floor of the Beit Alfa Synagogue are three beautiful and excellently preserved mosaics. When you first walk into the synagogue (which has now been turned into a national park and museum), you are greeted with a mosaic depiction of the binding of Isaac by his father, Abraham. On the opposite end of the floor, there is a mosaic of various images including two menorahs, two olive trees, a shofar and several other Hebrew symbols. This section of the synagogue is where the Torah scrolls were housed and read from. In between these two mosaics (which each deserve a writing of their own), there lies an undefiled depiction of *the Mazzaroth* (which the heathen call Zodiac); which also serves as a calendar based on the measuring of time written within the book of Enoch.

The mosaic shows a wheel within a wheel with twelve separate sections in the outer wheel. These twelve sections depict the symbols of the twelve constellations in the Hebrew Mazzaroth. The twelve sections also represent the twelve months within a year. Each section also lists the name of their respective constellations. Depicted in the inner wheel is the Glory of YAHOWAH, and four living beasts as described by the prophet Ezekiel, and John the Revelator. On each corner of the outer wheel, there is an Angel.

These Angels are of the Watcher class and are responsible for managing the dividing of the year into four portions (seasons) as mentioned in **Enoch 82:11**. *"And these are the names of the leaders who divide the four parts of the year which are ordained: Malki'EL (My King is ELOHIM), Elimelek (My ELOHIM is King), and Mali'EL (I am Filled with ELOHIM), and Ner'EL (Lamp of ELOHIM)."* While the Mosaic does not list the names given to these Angels in the book of Enoch, it does list the portion of the year in which each Angel is responsible for.

Each description starts with the word tĕquwphah (Strong's H8622 תקופה) meaning circuit of time or space, and coming around. After this initial word, each Angel then has a month assigned to them which represents the season that they are responsible for. The Angel on the top right has the word "תישרי" next to it which is transliterated as Tesheriy. This is the Aramaic word for the 7th month of the year. This tells us that this Angel is responsible for the Fall portion of the year. Enoch reveals that this Angel's name is Maliᵉᴇʟ. The Angel on the top left has the word "תבת" next to it which is Strongs H2887; transliterated as Tebeth and meaning the tenth month. This lets us know that this is the Angel responsible for the Winter portion of the year. Enoch informs us that this Angel's name is Nerᵉᴇʟ. The Angel on the bottom left has the word "ניסן" next to it which is Strong's H5212; transliterated as Nisan and meaning the first month of the year. This indicates that this Angel is responsible for the Spring portion of the year. His name listed within the book of Enoch is Malkiᵉᴇʟ. Lastly, the Angel on the bottom right corner has the word "תמוז" which is Strong's H8542; transliterated as Tammuz and meaning the fourth month. This infers that this Angel is responsible for the Summer portion of the year. He is named Elimelek in the book of Enoch.

While much more can be said about this Mosaic image; we can say without doubt that this is assuredly an ancient depiction of the Enoch calendar. This proves that as recent as the sixth century AD, Hebrew believers in **Yᴀʜᴏsʜᴜᴀ** were measuring time based on the writings of the great prophet

Ancient Mazzaroth mosaic at Beit Alfa Synagogue in Heftziba, Israel.

The 12 Hebrew Mazzaroth

1. ADNAR'EL (Tela - Lamb)	**2. YESHUSHA'EL** (Shor - Bull)	**3. ALUMI'EL** (Taomim - Twins)	**4. TAIMANI** (Sartan - Crab)
5. BERAK'EL (Ariyah - Lion)	**6. ZELABSHE'EL** (Betulah - Virgin)	**7. ELYASAPH** (Mozenim - Scales)	**8. SHEMESH ZOREAKH** (Aqrab - Scorpion)
9. GAD'EL (Qashet - Archer)	**10. KA'EL** (Gedi - Goat)	**11. HA'EL** (Deli - Water Drawer)	**12. ASAPH'EL** (Dagim - Fish)

Enoch. Daniel, when prophesying of the wicked nations and kings who would arise in the latter days, said that the eleventh horn (king) on the fourth beast (nation) *"shall think to change times and laws."* The Gregorian calendar in which most of the world uses to measure time is a direct fulfilment of this prophecy. This false calendar begins the year during winter where all of nature reflects death and decay.

Enoch's calendar, on the other hand, starts with spring when life is budding and beginning again. It is wiser to measure time in accordance to how the creator of time measures it, rather than following men. **Yᴀʜᴏᴡᴀʜ** is worthy of high praise for revealing these secrets to the saints of the latter days, and for providing us with visual proof and evidence to show that HIS Word is true. Blessed be He who sits upon the throne forever and ever. Amen. *Written by Jonathan Cordero*

JACOB VS. ESAU
יעקב נגד עשׂו

Siwan / May 2023 סיון

First Yom Reshon Sunday	Second Yom Shenee Monday	Third Yom Shelishi Tuesday	Fourth Yom Rebi'ee (Midst of Week) Wednesday	Fifth Yom Khamishee Thursday	Sixth Yom Shi'shee Friday	Sabbath Shabbath Saturday
	• 3rd Month: Siwan • Symbol: Twins • Mazzaroth Name: Taomim • Ruling Angel: Alumi'el TAOMIM = TWINS		<u>The Twins</u> The Twins are symbolic of the two offices that YAHOSHUA came to fulfill: High Priest & King of Kings. The two tribes of Lewy and Yehudah represent the spirituality and the government of Yisra'EL. These two offices become one again when YAH establishes the Order of Malki-Tzedeq.			
	1 Omer 30 Iyar 17	**2** Omer 31 Iyar 18	**3** Omer 32 Iyar 19	**4** Omer 33 Iyar 20	**5** Omer 34 Iyar 21	**6** 5th Sabbath Iyar 22
7 Day of Simon 1 Macc 13:51 Iyar 23	**8** Omer 37 Iyar 24	**9** Omer 38 Iyar 25	**10** Omer 39 Iyar 25	**11** Omer 40 Iyar 27	**12** Omer 41 Iyar 28	**13** 6th Sabbath Iyar 29
14 Omer 43 Iyar 30	**15** ☀ SIWAN 1 Renewed Month	**16** Omer 45 Siwan 2	**17** Omer 46 Siwan 3	**18** Omer 47 Siwan 4	**19** Omer 48 Siwan 5	**20** 7th Sabbath Siwan 6
21 🍞 Shebu'ot Feast of Pentacost (777)	**22** Siwan 8	**23** Siwan 9	**24** Siwan 10	**25** Siwan 11	**26** ✝ Martyrdom of Thomas Apostle of Yahoshua	**27** Siwan 13
28 Siwan 14	**29** Birth of Judah Siwan 15	**30** Siwan 16	**31** Siwan 17	<u>The High Priest and King of Kings</u> AND WE ALL OF US RAN TOGETHER, AND LEWY LAID HOLD OF THE SUN, AND YEHUDAH OUTSTRIPPED THE OTHERS AND SEIZED THE MOON, AND THEY WERE BOTH OF THEM LIFTED UP WITH THEM. WERE "TWELVE RAYS.		

Enoch The Scribe
& Arch Angel Uriel
חנוך הסופר ושר המלאכים אוריא

SARTAN = CRAB

- **4th Month:** Tammuz
- **Symbol:** Crab
- **Mazzaroth Name:** Sartan
- **Ruling Angel:** Taimani

June 2023

TAMMUZ / תמוז

First Yom Reshon Sunday	Second Yom Shenee Monday	Third Yom Shelishi Tuesday	Fourth Yom Rebi'ee (Midst of Week) Wednesday	Fifth Yom Khamishee Thursday	Sixth Yom Shi'shee Friday	Sabbath Shabbath Saturday
He Holds Us In His Hands "ARISE, LIFT UP THE LAD, AND HOLD HIM IN THINE HAND; FOR I WILL MAKE HIM A GREAT NATION." (GENESIS 21:18)				**1** Siwan 18	**2** Siwan 19	**3** Siwan 20
4 Siwan 21	**5** Siwan 22	**6** Siwan 23	**7** Siwan 24	**8** Siwan 25	**9** Siwan 26	**10** Siwan 27
11 Siwan 28	**12** Siwan 29	**13** Siwan 30	**14** SUMMER SOLSTICE	**15** TAMMUZ 1 Renewed Month Joseph's Birth	**16** Tammuz 2	**17** Tammuz 3
18 Tammuz 4	**19** Tammuz 5	**20** Martyrdom of Jude Apostle of Yahoshua	**21** Tammuz 7	**22** Tammuz 8	**23** Martyrdom of Peter & Paul Apostle of Yahoshua	**24** Tammuz 10
25 Tammuz 11	**26** Tammuz 12	**27** Tammuz 13	**28** Martyrdom of Nathaniel Apostle of Yahoshua	**29** Tammuz 15	**30** Tammuz 16	

Yahoshua
The King of Kings
יהושע המלך מלכים

Ariyah = Lion

- 5th Month: Ab
- Symbol: Lion
- Mazzaroth Name: Ariyah
- Ruling Angel: Berak'EL

July 2023
Ab / אב

The Lion
The Lion is King of all beasts and a fierce protector of his pride. In the same way, YAHOSHUA is King of all kings and invincible in battle. Without the male lion, the pride is defenseless and vulnerable.

First Yom Reshon Sunday	Second Yom Shenee Monday	Third Yom Shelishi Tuesday	Fourth Yom Rebi'ee (Midst of Week) Wednesday	Fifth Yom Khamishee Thursday	Sixth Yom Shi'shee Friday	Sabbath Shabbath Saturday
The Lion of The Tribe of Judah AND ONE OF THE ELDERS SAITH UNTO ME, WEEP NOT: BEHOLD, THE LION OF THE TRIBE OF YEHUDAH, THE ROOT OF DAWID, HATH PREVAILED TO OPEN THE BOOK, AND TO LOOSE THE SEVEN SEALS THEREOF. (REVELATION 5:5)						**1** Tammuz 17
2 Tammuz 18	**3** Tammuz 19	**4** Tammuz 20	**5** Tammuz 21	**6** Martyrdom of James Apostle of Yahoshua	**7** Tammuz 23	**8** Tammuz 24
9 Tammuz 25	**10** Tammuz 26	**11** Tammuz 27	**12** Tammuz 28	**13** Tammuz 29	**14** Tammuz 30	**15** AB 1 Renewed Month
16 Ab 2	**17** Ab 3	**18** Issachar's Birth Ab 4	**19** Ab 5	**20** Ab 6	**21** Ab 7	**22** Ab 8
23 Ab 9	**24** Ab 10	**25** Ab 11	**26** Ab 12	**27** Ab 13	**28** Ab 14	**29** Ab 15
30 Ab 16	**31** Ab 17	Hold Fast To Your Crown "BEHOLD, I COME QUICKLY: HOLD THAT FAST WHICH THOU HAST, THAT NO MAN TAKE THY CROWN" (REVELATION 3:11)				

MARY & YAHOSHUA
מרים ויהושע

BETHULAH = VIRGIN

- 6th Month: **Elul**
- Symbol: **Virgin**
- Mazzaroth Name: **Bethulah**
- Ruling Angel: **Zelabshe'EL**

August 2023

ELUL / אלול

First *Yom Reshon* Sunday	Second *Yom Shenee* Monday	Third *Yom Shelishi* Tuesday	Fourth *Yom Rebi'ee* *(Midst of Week)* Wednesday	Fifth *Yom Khamishee* Thursday	Sixth *Yom Shi'shee* Friday	Sabbath *Shabbath* Saturday
		1 Ab 18	**2** Ab 19	**3** Ab 20	**4** Ab 21	**5** Ab 22
6 Ab 23	**7** Ab 24	**8** Ab 25	**9** Ab 26	**10** Ab 27	**11** Ab 28	**12** Ab 29
13 Ab 30	**14** ☀ **ELUL 1** Renewed Month	**15** Elul 2	**16** Elul 3	**17** Elul 4	**18** Elul 5	**19** Elul 6
20 Elul 7	**21** Elul 8	**22** Dan's Birth Elul 9	**23** ✝ Martyrdom of Bartholomew Apostle of Yahoshua	**24** Elul 11	**25** Elul 12	**26** Elul 13
27 Elul 14	**28** Elul 15	**29** Elul 16	**30** Elul 17	**31** Elul 18		

Baby Yahoshua
יהושע העול

MOZENIM = SCALES

- 7th Month: Tishrei
- Symbol: Scales
- Mazzaroth Name: Mozenim
- Ruling Angel: El'yasaph

September 2023
TISHREI / תשרי

The Scales
The Hebrew word for scales is the same word for balances. Scales were used to measure out the cost to pay for something. YAHOSHUA used His own blood and weighed it in the balance to pay for all of our sins.

First Yom Reshon Sunday	Second Yom Shenee Monday	Third Yom Shelishi Tuesday	Fourth Yom Rebi'ee (Midst of Week) Wednesday	Fifth Yom Khamishee Thursday	Sixth Yom Shi'shee Friday	Sabbath Shabbath Saturday
"LET ME BE WEIGHED IN AN EVEN BALANCE, THAT ELOHIM MAY KNOW MINE INTEGRITY." (JOB 31:6) "WHO HATH MEASURED THE WATERS IN THE HOLLOW OF HIS HAND, AND METED OUT HEAVEN WITH THE SPAN, AND WEIGHED THE MOUNTAINS IN SCALES, AND THE HILLS IN A BALANCE?" (ISA 40:12)					**1** Elul 19	**2** Elul 20
3 Elul 21	**4** Elul 22	**5** Elul 23	**6** Elul 24	**7** Elul 25	**8** Elul 26	**9** Elul 27
10 Elul 28	**11** Elul 29	**12** Elul 30	**13** FALL EQUINOX	**14** TISHREI 1 Yom Teruah	**15** Tishrei 2	**16** Tishrei 3
17 Tishrei 4	**18** Naphtali's Birth Tishrei 5	**19** Tishrei 6	**20** Zebulon's Birth Tishrei 7	**21** Tishrei 8	**22** Tishrei 9	**23** Yom Kippur Tishrei 10
24 Tishrei 11	**25** Tishrei 12	**26** Tishrei 13	**27** Sukkoth Eve Tishrei 14	**28** Sukkoth Tishrei 15	**29** Tishrei 16	**30** Tishrei 17

Arch Angel Michael

שׂר המלאכים מיכאל

Kheswan / October 2023 חשון

First *Yom Reshon* Sunday	Second *Yom Shenee* Monday	Third *Yom Shelishi* Tuesday	Fourth *Yom Rebi'ee* *(Midst of Week)* Wednesday	Fifth *Yom Khamishee* Thursday	Sixth *Yom Shi'shee* Friday	Sabbath *Shabbath* Saturday
AQRQB = • 8th Month: Kheshwan • Symbol: Scorpion • Mazzaroth Name: Aqrab • Ruling Angel: Shemesh Zoreakh	SCORPION =		**The Scorpion** YAHOSHUA 's victory over death is represented by Him crushing the head of the Scorpion. When His foot trode upon the Scorpion's head, its tail stung YAHOSHUA 's heel. He had to endure death to defeat the Devil.			
1 Tishrei 18	**2** Tishrei 19	**3** Martyrdom of Matthew Tishrei 20 Apostle of Yahoshua	**4** Tishrei 21	**5** End Sukkoth Tishrei 22	**6** Tishrei 23	**7** Tishrei 24
8 Tishrei 25	**9** Tishrei 26	**10** Tishrei 27	**11** Tishrei 28	**12** Tishrei 29	**13** Martyrdom of Luke Apostle of Yahoshua	**14** KHESHWAN 1 Renewed Month
15 Kheshwan 2	**16** Kheshwan 3	**17** Kheshwan 4	**18** Kheshwan 5	**19** Kheshwan 6	**20** Kheshwan 7	**21** Kheshwan 8
22 Kheshwan 9	**23** Kheshwan 10	**24** Benjamini's Birth Kheshwan 11	**25** Gad's Birth Kheshwan 12	**26** Kheshwan 13	**27** Kheshwan 14	**28** Kheshwan 15
29 Kheshwan 16	**30** Kheshwan 17	**31** Kheshwan 18	**Treading Upon Serpents and Scorpions** AND HE SAID UNTO THEM, I BEHELD SATAN AS LIGHTNING FALL FROM HEAVEN. BEHOLD, I" GIVE UNTO YOU POWER TO TREAD ON SERPENTS AND SCORPIONS, AND OVER ALL THE POWER OF THE ENEMY: AND NOTHING SHALL BY ANY MEANS HURT YOU." - LUKE 10:18			

ABRAHAM
אברהם

QASHET = ARCHER

- **9th Month:** Kislew
- **Symbol:** Archer
- **Mazzaroth Name:** Qashet
- **Ruling Angel:** Gad'EL

November 2023
KISLEW / כסלו

The Archer
The Archer depicts YAHOSHUA, as victorious over death. He holds the bow and arrows in His hands. In the book of Revelation YAHOSHUA leads the 144,000 and the Heavenly Host into victory over the Dragon and the Beast.

First — Yom Reshon — Sunday	Second — Yom Shenee — Monday	Third — Yom Shelishi — Tuesday	Fourth — Yom Rebi'ee (Midst of Week) — Wednesday	Fifth — Yom Khamishee — Thursday	Sixth — Yom Shi'shee — Friday	Sabbath — Shabbath — Saturday
			1 Kheshwan 19	**2** Kheshwan 20	**3** Kheshwan 21	**4** Kheshwan 22
5 Kheshwan 23	**6** Kheshwan 24	**7** Kheshwan 25	**8** Martyrdom of Philip — Apostle of Yahoshua	**9** Kheshwan 27	**10** Kheshwan 28	**11** Kheshwan 29
12 Kheshwan 30	**13** KISLEW 1 Renewed Month	**14** Kislew 2	**15** Kislew 3	**16** Kislew 4	**17** Kislew 5	**18** Kislew 6
19 Kislew 7	**20** Kislew 8	**21** Kislew 9	**22** Kislew 10	**23** Kislew 11	**24** Martyrdom of Andrew — Apostle of Yahoshua	**25** Kislew 13
26 Reuben's Birth — Kislew 14	**27** Kislew 15	**28** Kislew 16	**29** Kislew 17	**30** Kislew 18	**The Arrows of YAHOSHUA** "YEA, HE SENT OUT HIS ARROWS, AND SCATTERED THEM; AND HE SHOT OUT LIGHTNINGS, AND DISCOMFITED THEM." PSALMS 21:12	

JUDAH
יהודה

- 10th Month: Tebet
- Symbol: Goat
- Mazzaroth Name: Gedi
- Ruling Angel: Ka'EL

GEDI = GOAT

December 2023
TEBET / שבת

The Goat
After YAHOSHUA'S confrontation with the Scorpion and subsequent death and ressurection, His precious blood became the Sin Offering for our souls. The goat is the animal that is sacrificed on Yom Kippur for the sins of Yisra'EL.

First **Yom Reshon**	Second **Yom Shenee**	Third **Yom Shelishi**	Fourth **Yom Rebi'ee** (Midst of Week)	Fifth **Yom Khamishee**	Sixth **Yom Shi'shee**	Sabbath **Shabbath**
Sunday	Monday	Tuesday	Wednesday	Thursday	Friday	Saturday
The Sin Offering "Then shall he kill the goat of the sin offering, that is for the people, and bring his blood within the vail… and sprinkle it upon the mercy seat." - Leviticus 16:15					**1** Kislew 19	**2** Kislew 20
3 Kislew 21	**4** Kislew 22	**5** Kislew 23	**6** Khanukah Eve Kislew 24	**7** Khanukah Kislew 25	**8** Kislew 26	**9** Kislew 27
10 Kislew 28	**11** Kislew 29	**12** Kislew 30	**13** WINTER SOLSTICE	**14** TEBET 1 End Khanukah	**15** Tebet 2	**16** Tebet 3
17 Tebet 4	**18** Tebet 5	**19** Tebet 6	**20** Tebet 7	**21** Tebet 8	**22** Tebet 9	**23** Tebet 10
24 Ascension of John Apostle of Yahoshua	**25** Tebet 12	**26** Tebet 13	**27** Tebet 14	**28** Tebet 15	**29** Tebet 16	**30** Tebet 17
31 Tebet 18						

SARAH
שרה

SHEBAT / January 2024 שבט

First *Yom Reshon* Sunday	Second *Yom Shenee* Monday	Third *Yom Shelishi* Tuesday	Fourth *Yom Rebi'ee* *(Midst of Week)* Wednesday	Fifth *Yom Khamishee* Thursday	Sixth *Yom Shi'shee* Friday	Sabbath *Shabbath* Saturday
DELI = **WATER** **DRAWER** • 11th Month: Shebat • Symbol: Water Drawer • Mazzaroth Name: Aqrab • Ruling Angel: Ha'EL			**The Water Bearer** When YAHOSHUA was crucified, His side was pierced and blood and water flowed out. His blood was the outpouring of THE RUAKH HA' QODESH (The Holy Spirit). The Water Bearer pours out His RUAKH into His Disciples.			
	1 Tebet 19	**2** Tebet 20	**3** Simeon's Birth Tebet 21	**4** Tebet 22	**5** Tebet 23	**6** Tebet 24
7 Tebet 25	**8** Tebet 26	**9** Tebet 27	**10** Tebet 28	**11** Tebet 29	**12** Tebet 30	**13** SHEBAT 1 Renewed Month
14 Asher's Birth Shebat 2	**15** Shebat 3	**16** Shebat 4	**17** Shebat 5	**18** Shebat 6	**19** Shebat 7	**20** Shebat 8
21 Shebat 9	**22** Shebat 10	**23** Shebat 11	**24** Shebat 12	**25** Shebat 13	**26** Shebat 14	**27** Shebat 15
28 Shebat 16	**29** Martyrdom of James Alphaeus Apostle of Yahoshua	**30** Shebat 18	**31** Shebat 19	**The Pitcher of Water** "AND HE SENDETH FORTH TWO OF HIS DISCIPLES, AND SAITH UNTO THEM, GO YE INTO THE CITY, AND THERE SHALL MEET YOU A MAN BEARING A PITCHER OF WATER: FOLLOW HIM." (MARK 14:13)		

REBEKAH

רבקה

DAGIM = FISH

- 12th Month: Adar
- Symbol: Fish
- Mazzaroth Name: Dagim
- Ruling Angel: Asaph'EL

February 2024
ADAR / אדר

First	Second	Third	Fourth	Fifth	Sixth	Sabbath
Yom Reshon	Yom Shenee	Yom Shelishi	Yom Rebi'ee (Midst of Week)	Yom Khamishee	Yom Shi'shee	Shabbath
Sunday	Monday	Tuesday	Wednesday	Thursday	Friday	Saturday
The Fishers Net "YAHOSHUA SAITH UNTO THEM, BRING OF THE FISH WHICH YE HAVE NOW CAUGHT. SHIMON KEPHA WENT UP, AND DREW THE NET TO LAND FULL OF GREAT FISHES." (JOHN 21:10-11)				**1** Shebat 20	**2** Shebat 21	**3** Shebat 22
4 Shebat 23	**5** Shebat 24	**6** Shebat 25	**7** Shebat 26	**8** Shebat 27	**9** Shebat 28	**10** Shebat 29
11 Shebat 30	**12** ADAR 1 Renewed Month	**13** Adar 2	**14** Adar 3	**15** Adar 4	**16** Adar 5	**17** Adar 6
18 Adar 7	**19** Adar 8	**20** Adar 9	**21** Adar 10	**22** Adar 11	**23** Adar 12	**24** Adar 13
25 Martyrdom of Matthias 1st Day Purim Apostle of Yahoshua	**26** 2nd Day Purim Adar 15	**27** Adar 16	**28** Adar 17	**29** Adar 18	**Fishers of Men** "And YAHOSHUA said unto them, Come ye after me, and I will make you to become fishers of men." Mark 1:17	

RACHEL
רחל

LEAH
לאה

Tela = Lamb

- 1st Month: Abib
- Symbol: Ram
- Mazzaroth Name: Tela
- Ruling Angel: Adnar'EL

March 2024

Abib / אביב

First Yom Reshon Sunday	Second Yom Shenee Monday	Third Yom Shelishi Tuesday	Fourth Yom Rebi'ee (Midst of Week) Wednesday	Fifth Yom Khamishee Thursday	Sixth Yom Shi'shee Friday	Sabbath Shabbath Saturday
					1 Adar 19	**2** Adar 20
3 Adar 21	**4** Adar 22	**5** Adar 23	**6** Adar 24	**7** Adar 25	**8** Adar 26	**9** Adar 27
10 Adar 28	**11** Adar 29	**12** Adar 30	**13** SPRING EQUINOX	**14** Abib 1 New Years Levi's Birth	**15** Abib 2	**16** Abib 3
17 Abib 4	**18** Abib 5	**19** Abib 6	**20** Abib 7	**21** Abib 8	**22** Abib 9	**23** Abib 10
24 Abib 11	**25** Abib 12	**26** Abib 13	**27** Crucifixion Passover Eve Abib 14	**28** Passover Abib 15	**29** Khag Matzah Abib 16	**30** Yahoshua's Resurrection Abib 17
31 Omer 1 Khag Matzah Abib 18						

Joseph יוסף

April 2024
Iyar / אייר

First — Yom Reshon — Sunday	Second — Yom Shenee — Monday	Third — Yom Shelishi — Tuesday	Fourth — Yom Rebi'ee (Midst of Week) — Wednesday	Fifth — Yom Khamishee — Thursday	Sixth — Yom Shi'shee — Friday	Sabbath — Shabbath — Saturday
	1 Omer 2 — Khag Matzah — Abib 19	**2** Omer 3 — Khag Matzah — Abib 20	**3** Omer 4 — Passover End — Abib 21	**4** Omer 5 — Abib 22	**5** Martyrdom of James Zebedee — Apostle of Yahoshua	**6** 1st Sabbath — Abib 24
7 Omer 8 — Abib 25	**8** Omer 9 — Abib 26	**9** Omer 10 — Abib 27	**10** Omer 11 — Abib 28	**11** Omer 12 — Abib 29	**12** Omer 13 — Abib 30	**13** Iyar 1 — 2nd Sabbath
14 Omer 15 — Iyar 2	**15** Omer 16 — Iyar 3	**16** Omer 17 — Iyar 4	**17** Martyrdom of Mark — Apostle of Yahoshua	**18** Omer 19 — Iyar 6	**19** Omer 20 — Iyar 7	**20** 3rd Sabbath — Iyar 8
21 Omer 22 — Iyar 9	**22** Omer 23 — Iyar 10	**23** Omer 24 — Iyar 11	**24** Omer 25 — Iyar 12	**25** Omer 26 — Iyar 13	**26** Omer 27 — Iyar 14	**27** Omer 28 — Iyar 15
28 Omer 29 — Iyar 16	**29** Omer 30 — Iyar 17	**30** Omer 31 — Iyar 18				

The Firstborn Birthright and The Bull
"AND LO, A BULL UPON THE EARTH, WITH TWO GREAT HORNS, AND AN EAGLE'S WINGS UPON HIS BACK; AND WE WISHED TO SEIZE HIM, BUT COULD NOT. BUT YOSEPH CAME, AND SEIZED HIM, AND ASCENDED UP WITH HIM ON HIGH." (NAPHTALI 5:6-7)

BILHAH
בלהה

ZILPAH
זלפה

RACHEL
רחל

JACOB
יעקב

LEAH
לאה

www.ingramcontent.com/pod-product-compliance
Lightning Source LLC
Chambersburg PA
CBHW040819120626

46551CB00004B/600